MILLENNIAL ROOST

Poetry

DUSTIN PEARSON

C&R Press
Conscious & Responsible

First Edition
1 2 3 4 5 6 7 8 9

Cover art by Rachel Kelli
Interior and cover design by Rachel Kelli
Copyright ©2018

ISBN 978-1-949540-05-5
Library of Congress Catalog Number 2018962041

C&R Press
Conscious & Responsible
crpress.org

For special discounted bulk purchases, please contact:
C&R Press sales@crpress.org
Contact info@crpress.org to book events, readings and author signings.

for Mom, Robert Carr Dubie, and all of *us*.

CONTENTS

INTRODUCTION

The earliest of epistolary poems in English includes John Donne's 1625 "To Sir Henry Wotton," which begins, "Sir, more than kisses, letters mingle souls…" Dustin Pearson's 2018 debut *Millennial Roost* is, then, a clear descendent of the form and the heir apparent of Donne's brand of satire. A poet in his own right, though, Pearson wants to know what the letters of his own book can do for a soul tied to the soul of a molester, a predator who violates even Donne's sardonic idea of "kisses."

Millennial Roost is a troubled, troubling, and troublesome book. There is no occasion other than adulthood, the ability to look back at one's childhood and evaluate what it has to do with feelings of lack that abound in the present. One such recollection pondering virginity leads to a poem that ends, "That first time what did I do?/And was I four or five?" Pearson's speaker seems to realize that he won't be falling in love or making love and that the desire for any of this is barred by the memories associated with Mr. Hen, an attacker named for his violent acts of cowardice and for his power to give birth to and mother the speaker's lifelong adversarial relationship to sex and sexuality.

Pearson's poems are necessarily allegorical, often leaning on conceit to reach beyond the individuality of memory toward a better understanding of the human condition itself:

> "Eggs are good for both laying and sitting.
> They are plain and elegant.

Let's be honest, we're all sitting on something
we're not telling anyone else, though we could."

As a poet, he is interested in epiphany, but he is in no way attracted to optimism. He sees his survivor as just that and doesn't expect something whole of one who's outlasted trauma.

Millennial Roost is never apologetic in its truth-telling or its disappointment at a world that goes on once such awful truths are told. How do we live through (and live on!) after violation? Pearson's surrealist vision is itself a metaphor for the lie that physical resilience saves us from mental anguish. But of course, a poet is not made by the darkness or the joyfulness of his content. Poets are whomever they are because of their will to take risks through originality in language.

The risk of *Millennial Roost* is also its achievement: dry (sometimes self-effacing) humor and palpable terror bind themselves to one another in each poem, "I beat the eggs. I use my strong arm. I whip those eggs around until they're perfection. I season them with the best intentions. This isn't the same shit you get day to day." Pearson stays flat and tells it straight so that we cannot question him having any designs on us: "I think my tactic is to do what hurts, reaching into myself where it's delicate or trying. I don't care about the risk." But he also stays flat so we cannot question the impossibilities that remain closer to truth than so-called facts:

> "I've seen chickens eat their own. That hasn't always been my practice. When I used to nurture them, they would hatch, become beings of their own and out of control. They'd travel, up the dirt road from the safety of our farm's enclosure to the border and into traffic, always to be run over. In the aftermath, I'd see them. Plastered to the asphalt. What to do, then, seeing how the larger world interacts with them but to take them home and ingest them…"

While the horrors of this book may challenge us, its voice is rye enough to enchant us: "Great, I thought, I suppose I still needed to be taught how I should be embarrassed." I mean that as much as these poems are anxious and anguished—"Make them describe it end to end"—they are also tender in their ability to dream of what Dustin himself believes unfathomable—"I've been waiting for you/and this closeness we wouldn't abuse."

What I love most about Dustin Pearson's *Millennial Roost* is that it questions our idea of poetic tradition (which so often seems to have little to do with the history of actual poems). It asks us what we mean by our expectations of beauty when life is so often ugly and clearly uglier to some than to others. It questions whether we've been misreading Donne and all the poets since Donne by having us walk with and watch a survivor attempt and fail to integrate into a world—a poetry—that expects only what ranges between conformity sublimity. And it quite smartly accuses us when we attempt to force him into a perception he could never have: "When I try hard enough it reminds me of a flower."

Jericho Brown

Atlanta, GA

MILLENNIAL ROOST

Jerusalem, Jerusalem, you who kill the prophets and stone those sent to you, how often I have longed to gather your children together, as a hen gathers her chicks under her wings, and you were not willing.

—Luke 13:34

Till Armageddon no shalam, no shalom
Then the father hen will call his chickens home
The wise man will bow down before the throne
And at His feet they'll cast their golden crowns
When the Man comes around

—Johnny Cash

PRELUDE

Is this the kind of thing that excites you? To be where words fall a body on the page? Where the expectations are coded and off-screen, away from wherever you've put yours? Perhaps in for something exotic, you've come where we all go to find it. Perhaps something impersonal or intimate. Maybe both. Something to tell you when you don't know. A body to work at a pace you dictate with the door closed. Is this the kind of thing that excites you?

Please, don't let me off-put you. Don't let me say anything that isn't true. I wouldn't know. I want to take you all the places you hope to go. People come with all kinds of cravings. Any lack found for yours might compel you to more of yourself, to ask more of everything else. You might struggle. I've known people to like that in the past. Is this the kind of thing that excites you?

I've cast my limbs wide with this. Maybe I'm searching for something too. You perhaps. I wouldn't deny that if it turned out to be the truth. I hope you won't ask me to do anything I wouldn't. It's all here for now. Stop if you'd like. Drop it. Move. Is this the kind of thing that excites you?

I've met several that suggest I dance naked and let them run their hands over every plug, pull and orifice, despite those I've left open. It's something I've done before, hope not to do again. I've been told to stop being so selfish. Is this the kind of thing that excites you?

You're still here. I'm sure at this point it's just you. Me. There's one thing I want to ask before we go down because it's deep. You've likely seen it coming. It's important. Be honest. You'll see things here I wouldn't show anybody, things I hope you won't abuse. No more stalling. Look inside yourself. Choose. Would that be the kind of thing that excites you?

BELIEFS

For the longest I've believed every man
will want to hurt me eventually.
I remember walking into this office,
lights off, with more than enough daylight
to see the red paisley rug at the center,
under the brown high back executive chair
catty cornered by the bookcase.

I remember wanting
to believe something else.
He was an academic. I'd heard
from everyone who studied under him
the brilliant therapist he'd make, and I thought,
better for me to work up to the real thing.

I sat, talking around the incident
that provoked my suspicion,
though never disclosing it,
while he stared and listened, the details
hollowing out his eyes. He never moved
his feet, even as the fit of his suit
pulled harder around him,
as if his body underneath was changing.

I could see the clenching of his hand
on the arm of his chair.
He kept silent, less opening his mouth
to ask information I wasn't offering,
and I think I knew at that point
what I'd given was exciting to him.

Maybe it would've paid to stay,
to learn what about the encounter, as an adult,
would make it different, able to see

each button of his shirt unfastening,
the belt undone, the buckle fallen next to his pants,
and the bulge bust open, the appendage stiff
after unraveling, the rest of him sitting pink
and white, a landscape for an early yield of wheat
stalked across his entire body.

MR. HEN

Scientists suggest that hairs
on the human body are merely
modified scales or feathers.

The feathers on chickens
are plucked from the body
with paraffin, or are singed.

I met a chicken once. He didn't say
much. He chased me to a closet. He showed
me around. He followed me home.

He taught me how the skin
on my back and belly lifts, folds, pulls
from the bone, and rolls like dough.

Each time was different, each time at the end
I told myself he was laying the egg.
Each time he was equal pitch, chicken, and monster.

I think I'll look him up.
I think I'll write him some letters.
I think I'll call him Mr. Hen.

LETTER 1

I've invited a lot of people to come on this journey back to the big purple building with the two white doors. It's not my intention to show them everything. I take them through the corridor all the way down to our stall. How does that make you feel? I thought I would only want to ask myself. It's like I need approval. Everyone else tells me what they feel before I can ask. At this point, the tour I'm leading is stopped right outside the stall door. They can hear us. I can usually get this far with groups. As the tour guide, I tell them I'll lead in. When I look back, before the door opens, I realize there isn't anyone who sticks around. What is it about this? Everyone comes in knowing the tale I'm telling, and what they'll find. They still leave it locked up and archived. It happened. I guess it will only happen here. Look at them. You should hear what they're calling this whole thing. Don't I need it? That's what we're really about, isn't it? Tell me that I shouldn't have to consider an audience. That when it was just you and me behind the curtain, you were able to get what you needed.

LETTER 2

There are all these reports out that detail the health benefits of eating chicken. It's often a huge part of the regimen for models in magazines and on TV. All of the reports mention how children love chicken. They can't get enough. They say it keeps you young. There never seems to be a shortage of chicken, and it also seems true that every old person would rather eat something else. I was driving home on the interstate the other day and saw a truck full of chickens. There must have been three to four, or five of them to a cage. They were all huddled up, each of them staring through the bars, but no one was going to mourn for them there except those with the wrong idea. I'm trying to find a venue for myself. When I was young, I wanted to be just like the leading men on television and in the movies, the ones who make the same impression when looked at straight on and in profile. Everyone seemed to admire them. Tell me, Mr. Hen, where exactly have you managed?

LETTER 3

I'm not a soprano anymore. I don't sing so openly. Hair sprouts densely from neck to thigh, but I clean up well. So many people make jokes. *Those sickos, they take you to the carnival. They buy you cotton candy.* I'd never let anyone make fun of you that way. I would say I was lucky. You would never use candy because that's not what I wanted. I wanted friends. You knew that. I don't know too much about this, Mr. Hen, so let me know if I'm off track. Isn't it true that when your kind takes kids to the carnival, they're probably not bringing them back?

FIRST KISS

He was training me to be revolutionary.
We spent late nights watching Al Jazeera
and eating hummus, me learning from him
what news without bias watched like,

and an appreciation for chickpeas mashed down
to a paste. We were like brothers. We
did the things TV brothers did, things
I'd never done, striking out in the night,

getting high in shadows outside cones
of orange light from streetlamps, daytrips to Wal-Mart.
He was the only person I'd known who could see a path
stretched straight out in front of him,

and I would've gone blindly even knowing I didn't believe.
You and I could never date, he said. That was a given.
He had a girlfriend I thought was good for him and it would never
otherwise be something I wanted. He'd said that in response

to some of the things I did, how I picked out produce,
other habits. What a strange complaint, I thought, the kind brothers
would never make. He was always saying he was an atheist,
that the cure for AIDS would have to uproot itself

from African soil in a syringe for him to believe,
and I didn't know then why that would be so important
to one whose beliefs required no faith.
We were at lunch one day talking about statistics

and world religions. He told me that of the world's many,
there was a good chance my faith was misplaced,
that he'd laugh after all to see me in a hell
with him. I think he must've been scared.

I was able to avoid him for years after that
until my 23rd birthday. I was drunk when I ran into him.
I somehow admitted I was happy to see him
all over again, regardless. He took my hand and kissed it.

He pulled me in, cupped my face, and I watched his face
come through the night, the alcohol, and the next morning
on the heels of every step of my long walk home before settling
on my lips. My first kiss was one I thought I'd keep,

it was important I reserve one thing to be intimate, but
trading it in made it all make sense. He'd asked me once
if I ever considered dating men. He didn't know how
close he was to hearing the story, how I never really consider

dating anyone, let alone with any kind of preference.
I would've told him I might've called that man a dad
or a friend at an age when I hadn't yet or just learned how
to spell them. If I could share that story with anyone.

LETTER 4

I had no idea I was implicating myself. I'd only meant to ask about you. I was on break at work. I thought I was joining an open forum started by one of my managers: *It's a chemical reaction between men and women,* he said. *It's the most natural thing in the world.* But what about... I started. When I went to work the next day, everyone was calling me a fag. Mrs. Cindy was still the gossipy-true-friend-to-no-one type she'd always been, still counting money in the office and smoking cigarettes. I think sometimes it would've been better if the question got me fired. That next day I was still to clock in, bag groceries, and run the register. The pig working in the deli asked me what I had been up to. He told me I'd been *kissing boys.* I'd never kissed anyone. I thought, this is how it would be now. My best friend Lindy heard it from her sister. In a text she sent me, *so you're gay.* It wasn't a question. She wasn't asking me. I was so naïve. I thought the KY my manager put in my hand was just a put-back, even after asking where it went, even seeing him and everyone around him laugh. I remember this one day when work was slow. We were all singing Elton John songs, so I didn't understand why my other manager decided to let me know he was sure of what he didn't know about me before. It was my first year working then. I understood by my second why Mrs. Cindy looked at me and laughed when her boss told her why he couldn't be a nice guy. I knew what followed must have lingered into my fifth year when the new cashier decided to share *what they say about you.* How was it that they knew? I didn't. How could I know what I was too scared to find out? How could I know that my brother would turn to me in the car one night and press me for an answer? How could I know that his friends were asking him that question? I tried to get it into my mind that I could tell them the whole story. I would start from the beginning, tell them about you and do my best to give them an ending. For whatever reason, I thought that would make it better, and afterward, they would realize something. I got a hold of myself.

BLUE JEANS, TOUGH SHIRT, AND AN APRON

I'm making dinner for some friends. I'm wearing my favorite apron. I look so lean and thin. My dad can't say a thing. I'm not much for dinners. I make mean eggs. They don't make a whole meal. They will satisfy. I crack the eggs one by one. I tend to them with my weak hand. I deposit them in a bowl I'm holding. When it comes to eggs, I have many skills. I scramble, boil, and fry them. I beat the eggs. I use my strong arm. I whip those eggs around until they're perfection. I season them with the best intentions. This isn't the same shit you get day to day.

The eggs are dank. I look good in my apron. It's blue with white stripes. I've got some time before my friends arrive. I retire to the restroom. I don't lose my edge. I need to cool down. I remember the pledge. When I feel a lag. I don't let it stack. I stop and do my best to get back on track. I play my favorite song. I stare into the mirror in the dark. The music plays on and on. I look so good. My hips sway. Left. Right. Left. Right. All sways to the beat. It's all eyes on me. Nothing can stop this. I extend my arms to switch it up. Lights on low while I'm on the rise. Hips sway left. Right arm down. I let it come all around. I have to hurry. Left arm down. Hips sway right and I'm making good time. I harness the music through my entire body. Express. Express. My dad isn't shit. No, my dad has nothing to do with this. Blue jeans. Tough shirt. I hear the cars pull up. I need a moment more. I grab my silver tray. Ready the hors d'oeuvres. Eggs in small portions. I make light toward the door. My dance modifies. It's much less labored. No free hands. The focus zooms. The hall narrows. My hips sway in a smaller space. I marvel. Look at the confidence I've gained. I twist the knob. I've got this shit.

AT THE KITCHEN TABLE

It's your treat
when your parents
start talking about the you
that you haven't been
for a while.

You're a big boy now.
Home for the weekend,
they don't expect you
to eat with them.
They don't censor
what they don't know
they're saying directly at you.

Mom looks up from the paper,
"They've arrested another priest.
It's hard to say how many." Dad
truly believes, "Those sick bastards,
just like the fags up the street. We leave
our children in their hands
and you see what happens."

It's admirable how simply
they understand and how little.
You think it may be enough for them
to answer the questions that keep building,
the ones that ask, "what happened to me?"
"what could I have been?"
and "where did I go from here?"

CHOOSING ABUSE

Tell the stranger who doesn't believe in anything
if you have to. I used to find myself in chat rooms.

I never went when I was sad. Forget your parents,
they're already taking the news harder than you have,

and never mind your friends. Neither your friends
or parents would know how to act. You've carried on

acting for so long anyway. They don't even suspect
it could happen to you. You'll lose with the truth

because it's not apparent. It's not an excuse.
Don't excuse anyone for what they've already said

because they don't know. It didn't happen, and you would
have to say a lot for yourself. Don't share. It's not right

to put yourself through any chance to show them.
You've been through enough already to offer up

what they won't notice has happened. What has been there
and again here. What all you'll see from all of them

after all of you have gone there.

SECOND KISS

I've begun to think of my body as an object,
and the chemistry between objects
more technical than romantic,
the smell of smoke in wet wind,
and how when the lights go dim
at the end of a long day,
the mood shifts. In this instance,
I'd want to ask him what he would get
from having his tongue knife at mine,
what he would take from the exchange
of saliva, what satiated him swallowing it.
I'd want to ask, what about it
could bring us closer than we'd already come
that day. I'd nearly given him my whole life condensed,
even going as far as his hotel room to finish.
He'd spent the day as a mentor, asking questions,
but I think again I'd been the only one listening.
We'd both been drinking, but if from my first kiss
I hadn't learned the lesson,
he was another that could teach it.
How you can't be friends
if the body is of any interest.
Can I kiss you, he asks?
I should be sharper than this,
should be able to say no,
even with all senses,
how to explain I don't see him that way?
I didn't say have sex, he says, but how
is what he proposes any different
when he takes my face in his hands?
I haven't finished my explanation
when he locks lips, tries to take so much of me
I wonder if after I'll be eaten. I wonder,
if I could just finish what I started

would he still have taken advantage,
but since he already had, I was done with him,
because I knew I could go forever
without doing this again.

PERVERT

You'll get mad when they say they don't remember.
You'll know that's bullshit. Make them give you the names,
and the faces. They're made by what they remember. You'd insist.

If something happened, they'd know how, and where they hid,
and be able to admit they might've just stood because they liked it.
What's not to like if it didn't hurt? It couldn't have always,

not if it went beyond a first. Make them describe it end to end.
The cold eased where that hand went, the waist
their pants fell from. Have them whisper what hurts the most,

how good their bodies still tell them it was, despite whatever it is
they've come to know. You'll need to hide how you'll shiver
as the warm air creeps from their mouths to your brain.

You'll almost be jealous, and so angry because you want a part
in how they punish themselves for what they still think,
how they take it on themselves to be in control of when it hurts

and when it doesn't, to lose every carried thing in a single moment.
You'd do well to wedge yourself in the middle. You'd be doing them
a favor. They're sick, too often they make that evident

in the sights and sounds they can't stand, the ones
that turn them in on themselves, and the ones they chase,
as if everyone was calling their name.

LETTER 5

You, Mr. Hen, are chicken mostly because you ran away. A rooster could never lay an egg like you did, would never lay as many eggs as you did without looking after them. I don't like talking about the eggs. Sometimes I feel like I hadn't paid attention to anything before then. You'd think I'd hatched from one of them. Sometimes when people confuse them for actual eggs, I giggle. I giggle so much I bend over. I curl myself into the fetal position, and struggle for breath until I cry. The endorphins do their job. They tell my body something I don't actually feel, and I dwell there in a haze, and I figure that out, too. People might ask me how I feel about it if they knew what happened. I don't think I could tell them. But if I were pressed to say something, I'd say it's kind of like that.

SONNET OF QUESTIONS

Do you remember those conversations
in grade school? The ones about sex?

Between cigarettes in the bathroom, by the lockers,
under the pullout bleachers in the gym?

Was everyone asked that question?
Why did it really matter back then?

Do you remember what you said?
Was it a simple answer?

Do you remember the stakes?
How big of a slut? How much of a man?

How far did he
need to go? How long?

That first time what did I do?
And was I four or five?

LETTER 6

I wouldn't say I'm being stubborn when I refuse the people who can spell out the kind of help I need. I don't feel I'm in any danger most days. I think it should be obvious who's in danger and who isn't. I try not to make a fuss about what I feel. It was only recently I realized how shady that could be. I was washing dishes. It was one of those rare times I let them pile up. I washed each one by hand. I didn't wear any rubber gloves. Even at that high temperature, the water gave the sensation of a second skin, the touch of another hand. Naturally, I found I'd gone elsewhere and even burned myself before I realized I was bleeding, all those damn knives I use, and it wasn't the first time I cut myself washing dishes. At first, I just stared at it. It didn't even hurt. Then it started to. There were so many dishes left to wash and I knew I'd just leave them dirty and unfinished if I stopped to dress my hand, so I just kept staring. It was all detachment and no blood. Then there was. The cut filled in slowly, then gushed. I could smell it, and I got sad I wouldn't be able to do that something simple I set out to. Most days I can't even admit to myself you were real. I go back and forth thinking what we did wasn't enough to count for anything, that there's no reason to be upset, that I would be fine with any excuse to be something other than dramatic. When I think about it how I usually do, I can only see myself, choosing, choosing like a child chooses between red and blue, vanilla or chocolate. Tell me, Mr. Hen, what would you call that trauma, when I get a little spacey and confused, and suddenly and completely detached from the body I use for the task in front of me? Tell me, Mr. Hen, is that you?

LETTER 7

Have you ever seen a chicken lay an egg? It can be violent. They get fussy. They scratch and kick up the dirt around them. With each push, they strain. They might moan or scream. Suddenly, from somewhere inside it, there bulges a veiny, red-fleshy ring. They push and push until something foreign to a pine palette starts peeking. That open sore of theirs stretches and thins as if to grope and slow the thing's momentum, to deliver it safely. The egg pours hot onto whatever cushion lies below where it will harden, and to think, this is a violence that happens daily or almost, and when a chicken might be sitting or eating grain. And the egg? I've seen so many of the chickens ignore it. The effort to bring it forward exhausts them and once it's here, some don't even turn around to address it. What way is that to behave? I've seen other chickens snatch and eat it. I've seen chickens eat their own. That hasn't always been my practice. When I used to nurture them, they would hatch, become beings of their own and out of control. They'd travel, up the dirt road from the safety our farm's enclosure to the border and into traffic, always to be run over. In the aftermath, I'd see them. Plastered to the asphalt. What to do, then, seeing how the larger world interacts with them but to take them home and ingest them, no different than store-bought chicken patties. I take hints from the chickens I see now, Mr. Hen. I go about my day in front of the TV, buying groceries, getting caught in the rain with friends, playing video games, and have them. When I'm ready, I eat them. I send them back in as close as I can to how I lay them.

LETTER 8

By now, I imagine that you've laid over ninety eggs. No need to tell me how many are mine, thanks. I picture you leaving a trail, a spiral road of yellow brick with thick ovoid bodies. Wouldn't something like that smell and expose itself eventually? There's little consequence in it for us. You've already made it past me, but there are at least three eggs I hold on to. The first is a practice in place, an exercise above and below the waist. Your hands fixed around my neck while your fingers slide over the face. The second, a threat in the same venue, an ultimatum I thought I couldn't refuse. The third, an exchange heard in kind words to my ears, but to everyone else would appear as absurd as two birds side by side flapping their wings. No reason to go beyond the third. Those acts are a blur. All I had learned from you by then was clear. I expected that we would fly. I guess that kind of trust is typical of children. At this point, I'd never board anything that promised to take me that far off the ground, but that's getting away from the point. I don't mean to beat around the farm. I've known for a while now that as a chicken, you can't fly anywhere worth going. You can't do anything you haven't already done and that's something I'm also questioning.

THE EGG

This is urgent. I've begun to run
out of metaphors, and I'm told the egg
in my work has begun to be funny.

It's something I've already admitted, but I need it.
Eggs are good for both laying and sitting.
They are plain and elegant.

Let's be honest, we're all sitting on something
we're not telling anyone else, though we could.
If eggs are jokable, we should all keep them

close, even the ones that are rotten.
They make children giggle
and seamlessly teach them about shame.

They are nutritious. They appear easily at breakfast,
lunch, and dinner. They can be added to cakes
and other sweets, and cooked over 100 ways.

I've laid them all over the house. There's one
under my pillow, my bed, on the mantle,
the nightstand, the stairs, in the window, by the TV,

the tub, the lamp. As long as they come,
I'll have them. It's unlikely you imagine
humans laying eggs as the hens do.

Something vital works up, through,
gets pinched at the throat, travels
all the way down shifting bone until it passes.

They make the most of your day
and remind you you're not in control.
This isn't a secret to them.

There's no mistake to be made.
Everyone's invited to watch me incubate,
but must also be willing to wait.

Don't ask me what's inside. Don't ask me
to scrap it before it hatches. It may never.
My department chair says eggs in literature

are used as a stand-in for gender.
I guess I might be ingendered, degenderent.
Ingenderent? An eggful to be sure.

I've learned to multitask. Laying.
Sitting. I've been passing one huge egg for years.
Much bigger than the others. I manage.

It protrudes. It's such an obstacle
at times. The pressure is so great
I can't completely close my mouth.

It has me walled up in fantasy
and buckling at the knees,
but what I do, I hope, benefits everyone.

I put an egg at every place that needs it.
One over my face so the skin
and muscles there stiffen.

The yolk runs down into my mouth,
runs out over my neck, lathers my skin,
trails my chest, caresses everything else above

the waist and completely eclipses the rest.
It's easy and harmless. Picture
the naked body with legs crossed.

At any human core there can only be a small number
of concrete things. Any curiosity fades when
the legs uncross, where all is laid bare and made ready

for critique. It's where I'll place my last.
It's there already, the egg and joke both.
One day, we'll all be laughing.

LETTER 9

They say if an egg breaks inside a chicken, it could kill him. They say not to reach in and help. We've both done some reaching. I understand you had to put them somewhere. You could've died. It seems natural to say here I wish you did. I don't know why it isn't. Maybe because I know it's a waste. Too late. I think my tactic is to do what hurts, reaching into myself where it's delicate or trying. I don't care about the risk. Not sure what that's worth, but most of the time, I can't even feel it.

LETTER 10

I have this recurring dream. It always starts with a certain feeling I get. I decide to stay home from school. All I can think about is how I behaved last night at the party. What did I drink? Had I been sensitive and said too much? Where did I go and to who? The questions come too late. The uncertainty gathers in an isolated place under my shirt, on top of my ribs. I start to sweat. It itches twice as much as it hurts. I know what it is. In a moment, all the skin on my body will be completely dry, but everything I feel on the inside will be otherwise. It feels as though I've been covered in lotion, stuck inside an old glove and forced to look through to the outside. I panic. I move my hand in a waxing motion on the part of my shirt that rests on top of the itchy spot. Direct contact with the skin and I know it's over. The relief fades. The skin starts to crack, the particles roll back and forth and collect into a ball I seize with both hands. I head to the restroom. In front of the mirror, when I lift up my shirt, the patch snaps then falls back like a noodle. The feathers that take its place protrude. They are white and wet. My acknowledgment of them hoists the rest. My skin explodes. The stray shreds of my self are everywhere, and when the debris clears, I look exactly like you.

LETTER 11

I've shared your DNA. I already share DNA with two people. I could consider it an honor. Do you know what something like that could make you to me? Do you know what something like that could make me to you? In one way, I've become a receptacle of the collected letting of your best intentions. I survive you. I've become something very ambitious in the attempted making. Biologists have their theories. Somebody with the right knowledge should've made you understand so you would stop. It didn't take. It would never. What a huge failure. What a huge mess. The reality dispensed. I still harbor it in phantom. Even today I get the two makings confused—on a date, while walking, when I'm lonely on the computer and see those silly pop up ads that read *find your perfect mate*. My knowledge comes in retrospect. I can't access the dual nature of whatever must have been. I don't know what I want from myself now, and the people on the outside? They suspect. They suspect the way I walk, talk, stand, think, dress. They suspect one of two things. They suspect one of two answers to the question. They pride themselves on assumptions. At best they are confused. I've already stated I'm confused. They demand the truth. They expect I know it. I only know that I still am, and that I'd be willing to let you off the hook if you could promise me I won't somehow find myself still looking for you in the end.

SEXUALITY

Who would have us look in the ordinary places
for the things withheld from us?

Whose hand could we be convinced held them?
Whose eye could remind us

the way we would look out into the world
from the blanket over our heads

to dreams we weren't yet made to force flesh onto
from the lot around us?

LETTER 12

Somebody asked if you were one of my parents. I wonder. What might become apparent to them then? In any case, I think it's a hideous question. I answer it simply and quickly: no. It doesn't stop me from imagining it. In a family portrait, I see you at the back, me at the front, the cone of an egg stopped short at the middle. Is that how that would work? Otherwise, you could be the front and the back, the mom and the dad, and the egg broken, its contents on the ground beneath you.

LITTLE FABLE

I called him Nagrod.
I covered my arms and shoulders
with my blanket.
I let the rest drape
a bold new skin
over me.
My arms spread
two scaly wings to flap
three stout gusts
before taking flight.

I mounted him.
I climbed up his back.
I nestled in his neck,
and we flew
so high up
to where no one should've been
able to find
us, inside
my chest of drawers.

"You always did this.
Do you remember?
What were you doing?" Mom asks.

LETTER 13

I didn't think about you for years. I thought about what we did every day. I remember it ended, or it didn't, it was just over at some point. I would sit down learning with the other kids with an urge to do powerful things, and it would get worse the longer I went. I think I knew the urge was violent, though that wouldn't have been a word I used to describe it. Can you imagine any kid let loose with and articulating those urges, observing them in a room filled with colored blocks and other toys between the orange juice and phonics? Can you imagine watching them trying to displace those tensions until the words came, and what about the look on their faces? With children, there's no tap, no way in besides the most confused and primal expressions. Why didn't those urges just remind me of the things I did with you? I would get into so many fights, so much trouble. I think back and remember you didn't even have a face. We stopped and you were still around, and you and the things we did disappeared. They crept around out of focus with no explanation, no clues except for how I was acting, and not even that for the hundreds of eyes that saw. I'm curious, what would I have said to someone if they just asked me to explain who you were, or how I knew? Do you think that would've helped? Were you watching for that kind of thing? I don't think we knew it would play out this way. I always knew back then I had gained something to hide. How is it something like this could have a fail-safe for staying hidden? How is it that after all you could just slip away?

LETTER 14

I had a thought recently. It took me back to my days working grocery. There was this lady and her toddler son sitting at the top of a cart. He was dirty, as if he'd been rolling in it. His mom had picked up a carton of eggs. I watched the kid work his way through the carton and pick one of the eggs to hold in his hands, and all throughout the store as his mom browsed, he kept it. When she was done, she came to my line to check out. I just stood there, useless, watching her kid, and the mom unload, eggs last. The kid's grip was still firm around the one he picked. Stupid, I thought. I might have been jealous. It was clear to me he got it in his head the egg would hatch if he continued to hold it. At that age, I already knew that could never happen because the thing inside was already dead. Did you ever do that? Look out into the world in the moment you were in and be forced to know more clearly than anyone should ever have to and admit you've already missed out on it? That somehow, without yet having your chance, the moment has been ruined? The mom reached for the egg her son was holding so I could scan it with the rest of the carton. He raised it as high as he could away from her and screamed. It's alright, I said, the barcode is on the carton. He can hold on to it. I thought, what would happen when it was time to cook it? Maybe his mom would forget about it, and maybe the kid would wrap it in a blanket and hide it under something until it went rotten and started stinking. Maybe the mom would pry the egg from his fingers because it's food not to go wasted. Maybe the kid would do what so many children do, drop it, have a fit, be devastated to napping, and wake up having forgotten about it. I know there are no guarantees, Mr. Hen.

LETTER 15

What we were doing didn't feel good. I couldn't think of a way to let you know that. I think I told you it wasn't fair. You agreed. You offered yourself to make it right. You got me involved. In my mind, I was just doing it back. It was different. I only ever used my hands. I realize now that was what you wanted, and I know that doesn't exclude me. I won't tell you what I say to myself every time I think about how, at one point, all of that stuff was normal. I don't care if I can't trust you to tell me the truth. I feel like a fraud having the last word. I've built you up to be something menacing, but I bet people would laugh at us both if they saw you. That's why if you were to call me a monster, I'd believe you.

LETTER 16

Who have you told? Would telling help anyone understand you? Do you have a friend who'd be mad at you for not letting them in? Or anyone who'd want to be that close despite what's been done? I told one of my friends just after the new year. I think I knew it was safe to tell her because I knew nothing would change. I've spent more time with you in recent years than I have with anyone else. I've thought so much about secrets and letting people in. We should open this up further and take all of the questions. There's only a small group out there who would want that. One thing about going at it this way is that we can work inward to what both of us will keep, what's not at all possible to share. If there's something remaining after all the questions have been asked, and no one is left speaking, we can call that our secret.

CAMARADERIE

I used to think of it differently.
I'd never talk about my childhood,
not even really when it was happening.
I hated group bonding,
sitting around sharing secrets
because it was "safe,"
because what a cheap way to know
what happened to a person
than the time it takes
to know a person.
It was a long day
turning night inside the bar.
We'd been drinking,
but not enough for what happened.
We sat staring at each other,
working up to talking about skin
and oppression, three colored faces,
invisible, included,
and I couldn't tell you what it was,
what trend, what opened
that broke the silence.
We spoke of boys and men
that had us, left us, that
never leave us in the night, sweat, and violence,
and where we couldn't find the words
we drew more of them,
held them in our mouths,
too deep and drunk with them,
choked on them,
spewed, out, down
the sides of our mouths,
to exchange them,
rub them on our skin
and on each other's faces,
absorbing them,
healing or beginning to
from nutrients.

RELAPSE

The doctor said she'd let me keep my dignity,
holding up a white sheet of paper for me to change
behind and place in front because her task was in the back,
simpler just to smile than decline her gesture I decided,
letting my pants slide,
rolling on my side to let her see them,
let her insert her finger so she could tell us both
what she felt inside.
She told me she saw two external hemorrhoids,
and felt at least one internally.
I told her my dad had been prone to them.
There's usually pain. Are you sure
you're not in pain?
I'd only noticed the blood.
I had to Google it, I thought
I was dying.
I waited to tell people.
"Stool" was always the word I used to describe where,
thinking it would make a difference.
Ewww, I'd been told, *TMI on the poo.*
Great, I thought, I suppose I still needed to be taught
how I should be embarrassed.
The resident at the doctor's office called it poop.
I remember the doctor said,
This isn't going to be
the greatest feeling in the world.
I know, I know, I said.
Once you get them, they never really go away.
I guessed then that they could have come back,
an injury I couldn't recognize back then
from the blood,
from the short walk home off the bus.
She entered slowly, gently.
I'd never felt more comfortable with that kind of thing.

I thought of my mom.
I'm going to prescribe you Colace to soften,
Metamucil to drink every night, and pads for the pain.
I think maybe this doctor didn't believe me earlier
when I told her I didn't feel anything.
I can't imagine opening to show my mom
the injury like I showed her every other
to interpret and fix.
Can't imagine any of this
being anything other
than painless.

LETTER 17

Let's do it all again like it would make a difference. We could meet some place quiet, play it out in fast-forward, slow motion, and rewind like we're watching our favorite films. Surely, there's so much we've forgotten. I've saved your seat, cleared away the space around it, peripherally isolating every detail, every possibility for something else. Even with all the time that's passed, I shouldn't be left to do this alone. This process is all about mixing the old with the new, and getting to something absolute. You see where I am. You're the only one of us that's moved on and to, but don't tell me you've grown. Don't tell me there's anything else you'd rather be doing.

THERE ARE ADVANTAGES

Having eggs affixed to the body at all the joints.
An egg sits stiff atop a neck on broad shoulders
that support it. You could put it down to rest
from the thoughts that spin and swish
and make you nauseous.

You could stick your head in the freezer
till the thoughts swell frozen against the shell,
then take your head out, watch the thoughts thaw,
watch them leak through the crack formed in swelling
onto the ground, on the sofa,
on the best date of your life.

It may occur to you in this condition
to run wall to wall around your apartment,
wherever, banging yourself and your limbs against them,
watch both become broken and splatter
with shell, blood, and yolk.

It's just that it would bother you
not knowing why you were doing it, or just to know
it doesn't make sense. The anger, lust,
yearning for destruction and displacement,
not enough to be the urge of the day,
and if you've lost control and find yourself
entertaining the episode in front of spectators,
it won't be enough for them, either.

Still, the slowly trailing mixture of your entrails
off the wall has its own meaning. You could make
your way out into the summer street, lie down,
transform yourself on the concrete from the beast,
the one that lets you do all the things
other people do with mostly invisible sensibilities.

An omelette, then. I believe even ordinary people
would recognize an omelette and be comfortable
with the trajectory of its cooking.
Those of the people walking along
would see you and spit, add other toppings they carry
in their hands and other places. Lucky you to be authentic.

LETTER 18

I think I talk around things this way so I won't be ugly. So that everyone will know the ugly, and know how, and know how it's not ok. It's so easy after what we've seen to be ugly, but this is how we must make beauty, Mr. Hen, by turning our back on every place it gets dark, by fitting it with a new head to look through, a head with one eye and one smaller, purer vision, and I'm not talking about you and me now, not just. We see things so differently after such an opening, and sometimes, because of it, we see nothing, nothing else, how a body presented to us can just be a thing when wanted, no matter where or how it's presented. We could promise. On us: no pricks of skin, judgment or gross entitlement. How when others are giggling uncomfortably at their small moments of discovery, we can choose between understanding and hating them. How it wouldn't hurt us to see our parents regressed and broken, not having them ask us but volunteering to part their legs and run a clean cloth of soap and water over where they wouldn't want us to reap them. We've been pinned. And the children, Mr. Hen, they're beautiful and ugly, too. The ones I've seen, you should hear the things they say, have said, grim and naïve and hopeful, and so ugly we gently turn ourselves and them away from it, because it's only then and way later we can see the innocence. That latter place I've skipped to unnaturally and gotten stuck, where from more wander and will wander to from a pairing like ours, and long after we've passed on. This will be for them and the yet to be them. You should come back and see, Mr. Hen, only that I no longer know the direction you'd be turning if you did that now. When I could see your back, I didn't know what to call it. The years have taught so many names, and between the moods, I think of the o, and the us, and the holes between them, but it's for the beauty, Mr. Hen, that I'm thinking of yours. When I try hard enough, it reminds me of a flower.

LETTER 19

There's this older guy I know who says he's been raped twice on two different occasions, by two different men, in two completely different seasons. I guess some people are just made for this kind of stuff. Aren't we different? He says he's been to therapy. He says all of the people there act the same. They're angry. They scream. Shout. They wipe tears from their eyes and mucus from their noses when they sit in the circle and share themselves. They are affected. He says every one of the people there has suffered a breakdown and that's how he knows this thing we have going isn't real. What we have going, then, must be exceptional.

LETTER 20

I'm sending a bouquet of flowers to our special place. I'm also sending the receipt. I expect to be reimbursed. Don't ask me the occasion. At some point, I imagine everyone has to decide whether each milestone or union is a cause for celebration or mourning. In any case, our culture dictates that they be documented. You're going to have to decide for yourself. The worst of the thing happens after you figure it out.

LETTER 21

I dreamt I was in love last night. When I woke up, that feeling was so heavy on and inside of me, I didn't know what to do. It's hard being that confused, and so immediately, I let myself back into reality. It was a great loss. Better to have that loss won in the dreams than out here in the open where loss makes a loneliness that gapes, that has to be maintained and concealed carefully so that it doesn't attract the attention of others. Out in the open, I keep meeting people. They're usually older, and I imagine them having the same experience we've had, only they're stuck in that initial understanding, and forward it in a way to younger generations that perpetuates the damage. In the dream, my lover and I had sex. We'd talked about all the things and there was trust and I believed beforehand. I like to imagine myself that close. And I didn't feel scared or guilty about it. Those are the possibilities. Sometimes I get a bad attitude and think I could go on without them, without thinking. You taught me. Sometimes I think I really understand how I've come to need things I don't need.

SEXUALITY

She comes over for dinner. I forgot
I asked for this date. I empty a can of corn

into my smallest pot and heat it on the stove.
I haven't bought groceries in weeks. I pair

the corn with white rice and soy sauce
and fix two plates. She looks beautiful.

We eat on the couch in front of the television.
I want to lie and tell her I'm vegetarian,

but she seems not to notice. She's not eating.
The steam wafts upward and nowhere.

I put on a movie, one I've seen many times already.
She touches my thigh. Her hand is on my thigh

at the edge of my leg. I think about shaking my leg
so her hand falls but stop myself. The movie is in the middle

and she calls me a name she's never called me
and keeps at it. I wonder why, but we're watching

a movie, so I stay quiet. She says something
about the way I look, but I look the way I always look

when watching a movie. She says I need a hug,
and hugs me before I can tell her not to.

The hug is long and slow and weighty. Her breasts
keep space between us but the longer we hug they don't.

Later, she throws her leg across my lap. My legs begin
to sweat under my jeans and I wonder if she can feel it.

LETTER 22

I haven't forgotten the embarrassment, chicken. I've gotten silly with this in the past, thought I could transform you endlessly, into duck sauce and peppermint, one of those new Frappuccinos with a candy straw, but no. I think people might begin to get you this way, and if not, they might at least laugh when I explain how chickens have no lips but are apt to cock. I mentioned their laughter earlier. I'll always try to make them laugh. I never want this to be funny. I can't make them laugh at you without making them laugh at us. So many of us have gone into hiding. So many have been found in the water, in and on the sides of roads, dangling in the open air before being taken down. For me it's this room I've locked myself in. Inside, there are mirrors, and in all the mirrors, you on and around me, and the scene. You're a growth. And for every laugh, the mirrors pulse and you pulse on me inside the mirrors until they shatter, and in each broken piece, again, the scene. The shards explode into the room where I've been staring and jet into my body. Before long, with all those that laugh, my body is reduced to the many shards that never stop playing the act of you and me. If you could imagine, Mr. Hen, looking down at your hands and seeing that, looking down at your feet, and all the people I meet that find themselves laughing at me no matter the time, context or reason, are always laughing at that, ultimately.

LETTER 23

I cried some today. It's been years. I managed right after taking a shower. I turned on my mini fan and sat it right in front of my eyes. I managed two big ones from each eye, but after that, all was dry. I'm pretty sure that's cheating. I'm not even sure one can call it crying. I knew I wouldn't have been able to otherwise. I've been trying for a while. I thought once I had the feeling in mind after the first one fell, I'd be fine and they'd keep coming. People use tears for all sorts of things. Sometimes, there's money involved. Some people use it to get back in touch. I don't want to be touched. I do want to get something out of all this. I know better than to settle for nothing. I'm going to try and be patient. I'm going to leave my fan running tomorrow as long as it takes.

SEXUALITY

When the world runs off with itself
into pairs, there will still be us,
unchanged. Our loyalty attached to its backsides.
We will watch them travel down the road,
past the bends where we've seen smoke, where
the lightning strikes, and we will warn them
that there's fire, shout from where we are
as loud as we can without notice because
we will be hypocrites if we have them taken
from that ulterior light they see in the distance.

We will have nothing but that sky-blued, lit,
green-earthen patch around us, and we will need to keep it.
We must hold back our hope. Our trek and theirs is how
the world will continue to work. They've showed us no one
invests this much and so closely in a body they can't run after
and touch, and best if only one so they might see it for what it is.

We know better, despite hurting over how a world looses
and breaks off into smaller ones. How it chooses.
We know we are how the world will have something
that lasts, that can be built back up from the worst.
They were here, with us, first, and if the only turn
is that we become abandoned, we will still see them
in the far-gone, untouched distance between us,
and when we perish, that hold will be there
should they ever need to come back.

LETTER 24

I want to tell you what I think I've given up. I want to tell you as if you were the person I'd give it to. I want to do this so you'll know who you are. What I'll continue to have to go on without. I think saying it will finally be what all this means. I want to tell you. I have to know first. I want it to be nothing. If I tell you now, I could lose everything. Maybe there will be time to whisper it to you right before it's all over. It's not over. I don't want to speak too soon.

TO YOU,

Cluck Cluck Cluck Cluck Cluck Cluck Cluck Cluck Cluck
Cluck

Always yours,

Mr. Hen

ADVICE

Tell them what it would look like and how it feels so they won't have to guess. Tell them anyone would do it. Tell them to scream, and that they won't get in trouble. I remember there were two toilets inside two doors at my preschool. An open space inside, they serviced two people at once. I was five with my pants all the way down. It was routine before a nap. It was important we avoid accidents. I wasn't the only one in the room. Bent over one seat I was asked to wait. "Relax," he said. It happened more than once. Nobody knew, not even after jokes in the dining room about the man on the news. In that room, I didn't see us that way. These days, I see us most often when I'm sleeping.

SEXUALITY

We would call it a kiss.

We would meet somewhere safe with our shirts off,
stretch our stomachs out as far they would go
and inch closer until they touched.

We would undo the zip of our pants, our noses
to hang over the opening there
until the scent changed.

We would use our ears as funnels,
pool the heat that lifts from our chests
over the other's nipples,
the warmth there warring with the cold outside
until the hair raised.

I've been waiting for you
and this closeness we wouldn't abuse,
a weight under which
we'd smother, stain dry, thin,
come and go silent and unspoken
as the spinning earth.

POSTLUDE

If I told you this was over,
would you be sad? Relieved?
Might you feel as though
you were losing something?

It's important. I won't be here when you are.
I'll remember my way back. Leave me
your letters in these quiet folds.
We'll keep each other.

ACKNOWLEDGEMENTS

Boundless thanks to Jillian Weise, Cynthia Hogue, Norman Dubie, Sally Ball, John Gosslee, Andrew Sullivan, and everyone at C&R Press.

Warm thanks to Ben Mirov, Josh Bell, Jericho Brown, Brandon Rushton, Jennifer Bartell, Kimberly Manganelli, Angela Naimou, Brian McGrath, Brent Robida, Jonathan Gates, Elizabeth Hatch, and Joel Chabrier.

Sincere thanks to the editorial staffs of the publications in which these poems first appeared:

"Letter 11" (formerly "Letter 6") in *Yemassee*
"Beliefs" in *Crack the Spine*
"First Kiss" in *Maudlin House*
"Mr. Hen," "Letter 2," "Letter 5," "Letter 7," "Letter 14," and "Letter 15" in *Blackbird*
"There Are Advantages" in *Noctua Review*
"Sexuality" in *Off the Coast*
"Sexuality" in *Pariahs: Writing Outside the Margins Anthology*
"Sonnet of Questions" in *Excavating Honesty: An Anthology of Rage and Hope in America*
"Blue Jeans, Tough Shirt, and an Apron" in *Metazen*
"Advice" in *Cahoodaloodaling*

C&R PRESS TITLES

NONFICTION

Women in the Literary Landscape by Doris Weatherford, et al
Credo: An Anthology of Manifestos & Sourcebook for Creative Writing
by Rita Banerjee and Diana Norma Szokolyai

FICTION

Last Tower to Heaven by Jacob Paul
No Good, Very Bad Asian by Lelund Cheuk
Surrendering Appomattox by Jacob M. Appel
Made by Mary by Laura Catherine Brown
Ivy vs. Dogg by Brian Leung
While You Were Gone by Sybil Baker
Cloud Diary by Steve Mitchell
Spectrum by Martin Ott
That Man in Our Lives by Xu Xi

SHORT FICTION

Notes From the Mother Tongue by An Tran
The Protester Has Been Released by Janet Sarbanes

ESSAY AND CREATIVE NONFICTION

In the Room of Persistent Sorry by Kristina Marie Darling
The internet is for real by Chris Campanioni
Immigration Essays by Sybil Baker
Je suis l'autre: Essays and Interrogations by Kristina Marie Darling
Death of Art by Chris Campanioni

POETRY

A Family Is a House by Dustin Pearson
The Miracles by Amy Lemmon
Banjo's Inside Coyote by Kelli Allen
Objects in Motion by Jonathan Katz
My Stunt Double by Travis Denton
Lessons in Camoflauge by Martin Ott
Millennial Roost by Dustin Pearson
Dark Horse by Kristina Marie Darling
All My Heroes are Broke by Ariel Francisco
Holdfast by Christian Anton Gerard
Ex Domestica by E.G. Cunningham
Like Lesser Gods by Bruce McEver
Notes from the Negro Side of the Moon by Earl Braggs
Imagine Not Drowning by Kelli Allen
Notes to the Beloved by Michelle Bitting
Free Boat: Collected Lies and Love Poems by John Reed
Les Fauves by Barbara Crooker
Tall as You are Tall Between Them by Annie Christain
The Couple Who Fell to Earth by Michelle Bitting
Notes to the Beloved by Michelle Bitting

www.ingramcontent.com/pod-product-compliance
Lightning Source LLC
Chambersburg PA
CBHW031150090426
42738CB00008B/1283